Bumblebees Can't Fly

"Bob Gannaway's *Bumblebees* is a light-hearted philosophy buzzing with good humor and helpful thoughts!"

—Harold Sherman

Bumblebees Can't Fly
(But They Do. And So Can You.)

Bob Gannaway

August House / Little Rock
PUBLISHERS

Printed in the United States of America
10-9-8-7-6-5-4-3-2-1

LIBRARY OF CONGRESS CATALOGING-IN-PUBLICATION DATA
Gannaway, Bob.
Bumblebees can't fly (but they do, and so can you).
1. Motivation (Psychology)—Miscellania. I. Title.
BF503.G36 1987   158'.1   86-28888
ISBN 0-87483-029-X

First Edition, 1986

Cover illustration and design by Byron Taylor
Production artwork by Ira Hocut
Typography by Lettergraphics, Little Rock, AR
Design direction by Ted Parkhurst
Project direction by Hope Coulter

The poem in Chapter Seven is anonymous. All other poems in this
book are by the author.

August House, Inc.   Publishers   Little Rock

To all those who made this book possible

Contents

Introduction

This is a simple little book. It was intended so to be. Its purpose is to inspire you to do those things we all know to do, but just get careless about doing—those things that will create excitement and happiness not just for ourselves, but for all of those people with whom we come in contact on life's journey here on Planet Earth.

There is a very beautiful song written several years ago called, "Let There Be Peace on Earth and Let It Begin with Me." The theme of this book might be, "Let there be happiness everywhere and let it begin with me."

I urge you to read slowly and meditatively. Look for ideas that are most meaningful to you, and then make them a part of your everyday life.

For many years, family and friends have encouraged me to write this book, and in deep appreciation of their constant encouragement—this is it.

As you join me in a sharing experience, my hope is that

you will find a stirring of memories that will bring a smile to your face, and perhaps a chuckle or two. You might feel a tear forming in your eye as you recall moments of deep joy or sorrow. Above all my hope is that you will be inspired to rededicate yourself, with me, to doing those things we know we should do, but so often fail to do.

If this simple little book can start a wave of happiness from me to you, then from you to those you meet along the way, who knows how many smiles will brighten dark corners, and how many discouraged ones will look up to the twinkling stars above, and with a renewal of spirit share God's love with all mankind. I believe that if we will cast our bread upon the waters, quite often it will come back "fruitcake."

A man was traveling along a busy highway some years ago when he noticed motorists in distress. Two well-dressed black women were standing beside their car, which had a flat tire. He pulled to a stop, got out, and offered his services. They expressed their gratitude and asked if he would mind sending a service truck to change the tire. He would have nothing to do with this suggestion. He took off his coat, got out the tools, and changed the tire. Then he waited until they got their car underway before continuing his journey.

Several days later there was a loud knock at his front door. When he opened it he was greeted by two men holding a large box. One of them asked where he would like for them to place his new television set. He quickly explained that he had not ordered a television set. They then asked if his name was Mr. _____. He said that was his name, but he had not ordered a television set. They handed him a small envelope upon which his name had been written. He opened the envelope, slipped out a little card, and read, "Thank you for making it possible for my mother to be at my bedside during my recent surgery. (Signed,) Nat King Cole."

Now you and I know what happened to that great entertainer, Nat King Cole, and we also know that this man did not go along the highway of life seeking an opportunity to change a flat tire so that he might earn a television set. No—he traveled along seeking an opportunity to be of service, expecting nothing more than the satisfaction of helping a fellow traveler in distress as his reward.

After I related this beautiful example of life as it should be lived to a group in Wynne, Arkansas, a young lady came up to me and expressed gratitude and excitement over my using this example. She told me that her uncle, who lived in Ohio, was the good samaritan who changed the tire and received the television set.

So, if you are ready, let us begin this exciting trip together, as we recall our memories from inner space.

Time to Listen

I'd like to wander down a path
From the busy thoroughfare,
And for just one brief moment
Forget each worldly care.

I'd like to pause to smell a flower,
To hear a robin sing,
To skip a stone across a brook
As distant church bells ring.

I'd like to sit there all alone
Wrapped in His loving grace,
Feeling a part of His universal plan,
Forgetting time and space.

I'd like to listen for His voice
That penetrates my soul,
That strengthens and restores my faith
So I may reach my goal.

Then when I'd rise, refreshed,
And go back to life's busy way,
I'd know that I'm a better man
To courageously face the day.

For I know I am never alone—
He is always by my side,
And he will support and strengthen me
Whatever may betide.

I may not always have the time
To leave my cares behind,
But I can find the peace I seek
In the recesses of my mind.

Actions Speak Louder

When my wife Anna Mae and I were on one of our overseas singing missions in 1980, we spent several days in England. While there I heard the story of three Englishmen riding on the tram.

One of them looked out the window and announced, "Oh, I say, this is Wembly."

"I thought it was Thursday," corrected the second traveler.

"So am I, let's get off and have a drink," chimed in the third.

Three men, of the same nationality, supposedly speaking the same language, and none of them understood the others.

I have spent over thirty years trying to become an effective communicator. I find that almost every day I say something very carefully and still realize that I have not been heard as I had hoped to be.

Several years ago I made a talk to the student body of a vocational-technical school in northwest Arkansas. As I was walking rapidly down the hallway to the front door to drive on to Fort Smith for some appointments, I heard someone rushing to catch up. Glancing over my shoulder, I saw one of the school secretaries. As she came alongside she said, "Mr. Gannaway, I really enjoyed your talk this morning!"

I expressed my thanks and then as an afterthought inquired, "By the way, how are you doing?"

We took several steps without talking, and then she answered, "Fine."

This reply stopped me in my tracks—not because of the word itself, but because of the way in which it was spoken. I looked her right in the eye and said, "You hesitated."

I shall never forget her answer.

"Yes, I did," she said. "Mother and Daddy are both in the hospital and I don't think we are going to get to take Daddy home."

She had said, "Fine," but obviously she did not mean, "Fine." The chosen word did not match the condition of her life at that time.

This experience reminded me that Catherine Marshall was absolutely correct when she said, "Every day treat everyone you meet as if their heart were breaking, for it might well be!"

Our ears allow us to hear the word—the sounds—but our hearts allow us to "hear" the feelings wherein the true message lies. So Rule Number One is: we communicate most effectively at the feeling level, not the intellectual level. It is not what we say to each other that is so important, but rather how our listeners feel about what we have said. A simple "good morning" may bring a ray of sunshine or a dark stormy cloud, depending upon how it is spoken and how our listeners feel about it.

Did you ever pass a compliment on to another person and get a negative response? I have, and it is very difficult to know what to do for an encore. What do you say after you express your sincere appreciation in the best way you know and your listener completely misinterprets your remarks? I wish I knew the answer.

As soon as I walked into the office of Mr. Floyd Pinkerton, the superintendent of schools of Havana, Arkansas, he said, "Bob, I have just been counseling a little boy who has been giving everyone in our district a whole lot of trouble. I do not know what I said to him, but he began to cry, and he sobbed through his tears, 'Mr. Pinkerton, nobody likes me.'"

He did not say *some* of the boys; he did not say *most* of the kids; he said, *"Nobody* likes me." This unhappy little boy might have been surrounded by people who liked him, but as long as he felt nobody liked him he reacted as if nobody liked him. I repeat: it is not what we say or do, but how our listener feels about what we have said or done, that counts.

A colloquialism used mainly in the South, where my family lives, is, "How you-all?" It is not the words, but the feeling accompanying them, that makes me feel important—that someone really wants to know how I am. If you have never lived where "How you-all?" is a common greeting, then you will not fully understand why I feel as I do when I speak it or hear it spoken.

A friend of mine came down from Chicago to visit me, and drove into a service station to ask directions to my office. A young station attendant ran up to his car and greeted him with a warm "How you-all?"

My friend thought for a moment and then replied, "I don't know, you had better check, I may be a quart low."

This is a good example of a speaker's intending one thing and a listener's hearing another.

We are told that much of our failure or success in life will come from our ability to communicate effectively. I urge you to listen with your heart as well as your ears. Look for the nonspoken communication signals, of which there are thousands and thousands. The movement of the eyes or hands and the position of the body are signals stronger than the spoken word.

If I tell a woman, "When I look at you, time stands still," she would appreciate it; but I must never tell her, "Your face would stop a clock." The literal message is basically the same, but the import is entirely different.

I enjoy the story of the circuit-rider who, after getting too old to make his rounds, decided to sell his horse and retire. He advertised in the local town news and a young man answered the ad. After a few minutes of horse-trading talk the young man paid the agreed price and climbed into the saddle.

"Get-'ee up," he commanded, but the horse did not move. He repeated the order with a little more authority, but the horse refused to budge.

Looking down at the old preacher beside him, he accused, "Preacher, you sold me a deaf horse!"

"No, young man, that horse is not deaf. I bought him as a colt and taught him my own commands."

"Well then, what are the commands?" asked the young rider.

"I'll tell you. When you want him to start you say, 'Praise the Lord,' and when you want him to stop you say, 'Amen.'"

"You've got to be kidding."

"No, try it," said the old man.

Straightening himself in the saddle and grasping the reins firmly, the young man commanded, "Praise the Lord."

Miracle of miracles, it worked. The horse sprang forward like the wind. Things went pretty well for a few moments until suddenly, as they were crossing a field, the rider spotted ahead of them a sudden drop of several feet into a pit filled with rocks. He forgot the proper command and jerked the reins back shouting, "Whoa!"

Nothing happened. "Stop," he pleaded and still the horse galloped on. Then at the last moment the young man remembered.

"Amen," he said, and the horse slid to a stop right at the edge of the drop-off.

The relieved young rider relaxed in the saddle, wiped the sweat from his brow, and, looking down at the rocks below, exclaimed in thanksgiving, "Praise the Lord." The well-trained horse bolted into space, along with his new master, to land with a thud on the ground below.

The same words do not always mean the same thing to everyone.

Listening is the other part of effective communication, and listening is an art. Most of us do not know how to listen. Have you ever tried to talk to someone and then seen from their reaction that they tuned you out? Frustrating, isn't it? The next time this happens to you, please do not take it as a sign of rudeness or disinterest. It may be, but then again it may not; it may be something entirely different.

In the motivational seminars I have been conducting for more than thirty years, I enjoy asking this question: "How long will a person listen when someone else is talking?"

Of the thousands of answers I have received, only a few have been right on target.

A schoolteacher at Mountain Home, Arkansas, thought that twenty minutes was about right. A lady at a Pizza Hut meeting at Memphis, Tennessee, suggested, "Forty minutes in a group situation." A personnel manager at a large manufacturing plant said, "Seven minutes," and a student at Caddo Hills Senior High School responded, "About twenty seconds." He was closer to being correct than anyone who had answered my question before.

However, none of these answers is correct. It is impossible to look at a watch and tell how long a person will listen when we are talking. Anyone who suggests minutes or seconds is talking about the concentration span, not how long a person will listen. How long a person can maintain an uninterrupted period of concentration can be determined by research and study, but we have no assurance whatsoever that a person will listen during his or her period of concentration.

Did you ever try to call your kids away from the television set when they were wrapped up in a scene of actors hurtling through space in a rocket? How long did they listen? You have to turn off the set or shake them to get their attention, even though their concentration span can be measured in minutes.

Earl Nightingale says in one of his motivational cassette tapes that the human mind can hold only one thought at a time. When I first heard this, I felt that surely I was smart enough to think about more than one thing at a time. However, after additional study and many personal experiences, I now know that this statement is absolutely correct. Your mind and mine can hold only one thought at a time.

In 1980, I attended a conference in Kansas City

sponsored by Kentucky Fried Chicken, and as I was flying home I took out the airline's magazine from the rack to pass the time. An article on memory caught my attention and I was amazed to read that memory experts now believe that at age seventy the human mind can store over three trillion items. So when we say that the mind can hold only one thought at a time, we are not referring to the storage area of our minds—the subconscious—but only our immediate, conscious thought. (The subconscious will be discussed more fully in a later chapter.) If we could sell each item stored in the mind of just one seventy-year-old for a dollar, we could retire the national debt, and do all the wonderful things that need to be done for the sick and hungry of the world. Therefore, I repeat, with all the vast knowledge stored in our subconscious minds, we can hold only one of these thoughts before our attention at a time.

You can think of your mind as a slide projector. Its tray might contain a hundred slides, but they can be shown on the screen only one at a time. For example, a thought about twins is a single thought—two individuals, but one thought. If we concentrate on one, the image of the other necessarily leaves the mind. You can take a picture of them and project that picture on the screen in your living room or on the screen of your mind, but they can be projected on that screen only one at a time.

A Cajun mother gave birth to twins, a boy and a girl. The family had difficulty thinking of names for the new arrivals. Uncle Louie heard of the problem and volunteered to suggest some names. In desperation they gave him the job, even though Uncle Louie seemed to be baffled by the simplest of things. Several months later the cousins were talking and one asked the other, "How are the twins doing?"

The second answered that they were doing just fine

and that Uncle Louie had named them. Anxious to know what he had come up with, the first cousin asked, "Well, what did Uncle Louie name them?"

"He named the little girl Denise," was the reply.

"That's a nice name. What did he name the little boy?"

"De nephew," came the reply.

Not the best of names, perhaps, but Uncle Louie got the job done. The point is that regardless of the names we can think of only one thing at a time—twins being a single thought.

In 1981 AETN, the educational channel in Conway, Arkansas, was conducting its annual fundraising drive. During the telecasting they continued to transmit their regular programs most of the time. In order to give credit to their supporters, they would project the names of the contributors on a tape that moved across the bottom of the screen. I found that I could listen to the program or read the names but could not do both at the same time. When reading the names I could see changing scenes and hear words or music, but I could not relate to the program. When I began to listen to the program, I could see letters moving across the screen but could not comprehend the names. My mind could move very quickly from one to the other and back again, but I could relate to only one at a time.

I made this observation to a group of bank employees at a meeting in Van Buren, Arkansas, and one of the bank tellers said, "You know, I never thought about it, but I can't whistle and count money accurately at the same time."

So here is Rule Number Two, which so few of us really understand: a person will listen just so long as what is being said is more interesting than what he is thinking.

Let us play with this idea for a while. Please clear your mind for a moment and use your imagination to paint a mental picture as clearly as possible of the following situation: *The little girl ran into the street just as the car turned the corner.*

As soon as you have a clear picture of this incident, answer these questions:

How old is the little girl? (Five is the age most often given.)

What color is her hair?

What color is her dress? (Red and blue are the colors most often given.)

And now, the most important question of all—what color is the automobile that turns the corner just as the little girl runs into the street?

Please do not read on until you have answered all of the above questions in your mind.

The color most often given for the automobile is black, and I have found that the older the person answering, the most likely it is that he will picture a black car. I believe that one of the reasons most of us see a black car is that we do not know what to expect, and we have a fear of something harming the little girl. The things you and I fear are the things we do not understand. A move to a new location, a new job, a new club, a sudden physical pain, a child who does not come home on time—any of these can fill us with uncertainty about what is going to happen, building tension in us and often overwhelming us with negative thoughts.

I have created in your mind a very serious situation that could be similar to one you are facing now or have recently faced. Since I created this one, let me "change slides" so that we can move on together:

The beautiful little five-year-old blond girl, wearing

her new red dress, ran into the street just as her father turned the corner in his gold car to pick her up and take her down the street to Billy Johnson's birthday party.

Is your mental picture now more positive? Then we can move on.

Much has been written and said about positive thinking. Since we can focus on only one thought at a time, let us strive to push out negative thoughts and replace them with happy, positive ones. Let us learn to expect the best in people and situations.

Driving to one of my appointments, I had a thought so strong that I pulled over to the side of the road and wrote it down. I do not claim that it is original; I only know that I do not recall having heard or read it. This is what I wrote: *I had rather be wrong expecting the best than to be right expecting the worst.* Just another reminder that we need to develop the habit of thinking positively.

"Come here a minute," called the mother to her young son. "Go out on the back porch and bring me the broom."

"But, Mommy, it's dark out there," protested her son, "and I'm afraid of the dark."

"There is no need for you to be afraid of the dark," reassured his mother. "There's only God out there."

The little boy went to the back door, opened it a wee bit, and placed his mouth in the opening to make his earnest request. "God," he pleaded, "if you're out there, hand me the broom."

Not understanding what the mother already knew, the little boy was afraid.

Actions do speak louder than words. It is not always what we say, but most often what we fail to say or do, that conveys a true message.

When we are listeners, let us make the person talking to us feel important by giving him or her our undivided attention. We might learn something new and exciting. It is worth a try, and if we are willing to listen, who knows—the next time we speak we might find an interested listener ourselves.

Remember, then:

Rule 1. We communicate most effectively at the feeling level, not the intellectual level; and

Rule 2. People will listen just so long as what we are saying is more interesting than what they are thinking.

Dear Reader,

Please turn and read page 51
for page 25 and vice versa. We
regret the mix-up.

Where Are You Going?

Do you know where you are going? Do you know where you want to be next year, five years from now, or ten years from now? If you don't, how can anyone help you get anywhere? People do not have a difficult time *reaching* their goals; it is *establishing* them that creates a problem. Once goals are firmly set, then in most cases they will be obtained.

Another of Earl Nightingale's messages contains the statement that the world doesn't care whether we fail or succeed. The first time I heard this I felt the world was against me. Then after hearing it several times, I realized that the statement is true. Were you ever in a schoolroom where there was a teacher's pet? Have you ever worked where favoritism was being shown? It was no fun, right?—unless you were the teacher's pet or the one receiving the favors. So the world does not play favorites, and that is as it should be. We must choose our goals and day and haven't found something to laugh about during that day, I challenge you to stand in front of a mirror and laugh at yourself. It may be difficult at first, but if you persist, soon you will reap the benefits and rewards of a richer, fuller life. Some who have tried this technique have later reported that it worked for them, and it will work for you as well.

Anna Mae and I attended a school program for our older daughter, Diane, many years ago. Seated in the auditorium of Jefferson Elementary School, we were being entertained by some of the students.

Onto the stage came a little boy with red hair parted down the middle and so many freckles that if he had had just one more he would have had to hold it in his hand, for there was no more room for it on his little face. He was grinning from ear to ear. I was so moved by his happy expression, I turned to Anna Mae and said, "Isn't that a cute grin?"

Before she could answer, one of his teachers tapped me on the shoulder and said with resignation in her voice, "Yep, and it saved his life a dozen times this year."

You see what I mean, don't you? We will be healthier—and perhaps safer—if we develop a good, clean sense of humor.

I was associated for a brief period of time with a doctor by the name of Yandell. I do not recall his first name. During the day we spent together he shared many interesting things with me, and one of these was that doctors very seldom find stomach ulcers in a person who smiles a lot. This is dramatic evidence that laughter can be very beneficial to our health.

The other reason that I challenge you to develop an ability to laugh is this: there are going to be days when even the most optimistic and positive-thinking person will feel that no one cares and that he is worthless and unloved, and will begin to doubt himself and others. It is then that we need to be able to roll with the punch, to pick ourselves up, dust ourselves off, and, with a little laughter, start over again. The person who needs our smiles is the one who does not have one to give. Let us seek out that lonely one and make him know that we care.

We may not be responsible for *being* down, but we are responsible for *staying* down.

Attitudes Make the Difference

I am told that there are three signs of old age; the first is the loss of memory, and I can't remember the other two.

The older we get the worse it gets. A man went to his doctor and told him he was having trouble remembering anything from one minute to the next.

"How long have you had this problem?" inquired the doctor.

"What problem?" was the confused reply.

I shall never forget what our science teacher told us when I was in grammar school. She said, "Children, scientists have measured the height and weight of the bumblebee's body as opposed to the tensile strength and area of coverage of its wings, and, scientifically speaking, a bumblebee cannot fly." According to her this is a scientific fact. Aren't we glad that no one has told the bumblebee! It does not walk but flies from flower to flower pollinating plants so we can enjoy the beauty of nature all around us.

I am convinced that you and I can fly to undreamed heights if we will just remove the mental barriers placed upon our own ability by our negative thinking and "fly."

Whenever I ask my listeners this question, I know what the answer will be, because except for one misunderstanding of the question at a meeting in Memphis, it is always the same.

When I ask, "Do you believe that everyone is improvable?" the answer is always a resounding *"Yes"* or *"Certainly."*

The only time I received a negative response was from a lady who said that she did not agree. At break time I approached her and asked if she really did not believe that people are improvable. Her answer indicated that she had not understood the question, for she told me very quickly that she thought I had asked if people *would* improve. Then when I repeated the question, she responded that she did believe that people are improvable.

This reminded me of an old farmer, who was plowing in his field one hot, dusty summer day when he was approached by a young, enthusiastic county agricultural agent.

"Brother Jones," asked the county agent, "do you plan to be home Saturday?"

"I expect so, young man. Why?"

"Well, Brother Jones, I would like to come out and show you how to get more production out of your land."

"Ain't no need in you comin'," said the old farmer, turning back to his chores, "I ain't plowin' half as good as I know how to now."

So, while everyone is improvable, you and I know that not everyone will get his "want-to" in order and improve.

I am indebted to a school superintendent in southwest Arkansas for sharing something with me that happened to him while he was a boy, which turned his life around. This man holds two college degrees, so you know how many years he spent in the "halls of ivy." But he told me that the most valuable lesson he learned all the way through school was from an eighth-grade teacher. She did not tell him to study harder; she did not chastise him for skipping classes; she simply told him, "Son, all you need to do is get your 'want-to' in order."

Volunteer work in the public schools is very challenging and satisfying work for me. I wish you could sit with me in one of the sessions as these wonderful young boys and girls suddenly spread their wings and begin to fly. Oh, it is not always easy to get them to listen. I found out many years ago that only when I can convince them that I love them—not necessarily for what they are doing or have done, but for what they can become—and only when I can get them to believe that they can fly regardless of what they have been told will wonderful things begin to happen.

I was so inspired by one group that I wrote the following poem and dedicated it to them. Now I share a copy with each young person in my classes.

Scientists tell us a bumblebee can't fly;
He's much too fat and his wings too small;
And everyone knows with things like that
He can't get off the ground at all.

But you see no one ever told the bumblebee,
And, not knowing that it can't be done,
He spreads his wings and lifts his weight
Triumphantly toward the sun.

Has anyone ever told you that you cannot fly?
Or worse still, have you told yourself these things
Without spreading your wings and rising up,
Feeling the joy that accomplishment brings?

You *can* fly if you believe you can,
For, you see, bumblebees do,
And if the tiny bumblebee can do it,
So can *you* and *you* and *you*.

Now that we are in agreement that people are improvable, let us consider some of those things we can do each day that we are not doing, or not doing as well as we could—things that will help us fly a little higher.

Smiling

Putting on the appropriate clothing is the way we dress for the different activities in which we are engaged—proper clothing for a particular event; but I am convinced that regardless of how well and appropriately we are attired, we are not completely dressed until we put a smile on our faces. We are told that it takes only 13 muscles to smile, while it takes as many as 82 to frown. So, you see, we can save energy and spread sunshine by a simple, sincere smile.

A salesman friend of mine said he started out to work one morning and his four-year-old son asked, "How are you feeling this morning, Daddy?"

"Just great," was the father's reply.

"You haven't notified your face yet, have you?" admonished the little boy.

What's going on in the inside shows on the outside.

If you are married and want to get a little extra attention at home, just go to bed, curl up to go to sleep, and smile. Don't say a word, just smile.

Appreciation

The deepest craving of an individual is to be needed, to feel important and appreciated. Many surveys point out that sincere appreciation is one of the most effective motivators. Money or material reward ranks far down most lists.

We have dear friends in south Arkansas, Harold and Alice Reid. Harold is the president of the bank there, and Alice devotes many hours each year to the Junior Miss pageants.

Several years ago they took their two daughters, Gay and Joy, into a restaurant in Little Rock. Little Joy was a preschooler and couldn't read, but the wise waitress gave her a menu as she did to everyone else at the table. Joy opened it, studied it for a moment, and then, looking up at her mother, exclaimed excitedly, "Hey, look, Mommy, she thinks I'm people."

The waitress had made Joy feel important, and she responded.

My health has been very good, for which I am grateful, so when I went into the doctor's office one day it was on business rather than as a patient. He was occupied, so I sat for a few minutes in his waiting room. Picking up a magazine, I noticed an article that related the story of an older couple in a hospital room. She was in bed and he sat beside her. The doctors had just left after giving them the medical prognosis: her disease was terminal.

In the lonesomeness of that little room, he turned to

his companion of many years and said, "Honey, you can't die. I need you."

In a weakened voice she responded, "That's the first time you have ever told me."

I do not know if this dear soul is alive now or not, but the balance of the report said that she did get out of bed, she did go home, and she did live because someone needed her. How true it is—we all need somebody or we are nobody! There is a beautiful sequel to this story. The older couple was returning home one evening, driving up the lane in their little pickup truck. He was holding the wheel firmly with both hands, doing his best to dodge the potholes, and she was leaning out her window with one elbow partially ouside. Looking up at the full moon glowing softly through the gently swaying pine trees, she sighed deeply, turned to her husband, and asked, "Paw, you 'member when we first got married how I used to set over so close to you and we'd cuddle and have so much fun?"

Without taking his eyes off the road or his hands off the wheel he responded, "Maw, I ain't moved." It takes two.

When I was praticing law I found that when parties drew up a fifty-fifty contract they did not always agree on what 50 percent was. A successful marriage is not where two people look at each other; I believe a successful marriage is a relationship where two people look together in the same direction.

Do you have children who argue about who gets the biggest piece of the apple or the largest slice of cake? You might try this. Let one of the children cut the apple in two and the other have first choice. This is about as even as you will ever get it. If there is a child in your neighborhood who won't go home on time, you might say to him, "Junior, when you get ready to go home, I have some

34

cookies I want you to take with you." It works wonders when we add a little bit of sugar to the medicine.

Faith

Have you ever gone into a strange meeting-place and checked the chair before you sat down? Have you ever sat at a table in a restaurant where you have never been before and watched the other patrons eat before picking up your own fork and starting to eat? Have you ever gone into a strange office or apartment building and watched others ride the elevator a few times before you gained enough courage to step inside and push the button to the desired floor? Obviously I am speaking of faith or rather the lack of it in these instances. We must have faith in those who make the chairs, prepare the food, or maintain the elevators if we are to move harmoniously through life. If we had to stop and question everything every day, just imagine the complete chaos that would engulf us.

Speaking of elevators, Uncle Bill came to "the big city" for the first time and was being shown the sights by his nephew. As they stood in front of the tall buildings, Uncle Bill studied one of them from the sidewalk to its top story reaching into the sky. Turning to his nephew, he observed, "They could put a lot of corn in that one."

"Uncle Bill," exclaimed his nephew, "that's not a silo—that's a place where people work."

"Sure 'nuf?" asked Uncle Bill.

"Yes, would you like to see inside?"

"I sure would."

They walked into the busy lobby and watched as people rushed into the elevators and then rushed out again when the doors opened. Uncle Bill was awestruck.

In a few minutes a small fat lady got into an elevator

and the doors closed behind her. She was one of those women described by a comedian who said, "You can get rid of fat, but you can't get rid of ugly." She had both problems.

In a few minutes this same elevator door opened and out came a beautiful young woman. As she walked briskly by, Uncle Bill could not believe his eyes.

Suddenly he took off in a dead run, with his nephew trying to catch up. "Where are you going, Uncle Bill?" cried his puzzled nephew.

Without pausing Uncle Bill called back, "Oh, I'm going down to the farm and fetch ole Bessie and throw her in that box." This is faith in action.

I must admit to you that whenever I feel things are getting out of hand, I have a tendency to blame others for my failures. All the while I know that I am responsible for my thoughts and actions. Life is a lot less complicated when I accept the responsibility for my actions and try to see what lessons I can learn from each experience and then move on. When something goes wrong in our lives, we should pause and seek the cause. Altering or eliminating the cause will alter or eliminate the effect.

There was a man in a bar who finally realized that they could make it a lot faster than he could drink it, so he gave up. Propping himself in the corner of the bar, he went to sleep. A practical joker walked up and saw an opportunity to have a little fun. He took some limburger cheese off a platter and gently rubbed it under the sleeper's nose. He then took a seat nearby to see what would happen. He did not have to wait long. In a few minutes the inebriate sniffed a few times, blinked his eyes, and, pulling himself up, made his way out the door for a breath of fresh air. He wasn't gone long, however, for he came staggering back in and announced in a loud voice, "It ain't no use, fellows, the whole world stinks."

Where is the problem? Is is within us or in the world? Obviously a little soap and water would have cleared the air and eliminated the problem.

Several years ago I cut out of the *Saturday Evening Post* a poem that illustrates what I am trying to say. Whoever wrote the verse complained that the man across the street should paint his house; that the lady on one side let her kids run around in dirty clothes all the time; and that the man on the other side never washed his automobile. The poem ended with a thought that went something like this: "I found that when I washed the windows of my own house, everything in the neighborhood cleared up."

Wouldn't it be nice if, when we have those dark, negative thoughts, when we have a tendency to blame others for our failures, we would just stop and emotionally wash the windows of our own houses so we could look into the neighborhood with a clear vision?

Let us keep our faith alive and vital—faith in God, faith in ourselves, and faith in our fellow man.

Faith is the bird that feels the dawn and sings before the darkness is gone.

We know that after the tears come smiles
And after the drought, the rain.
We learn fully to appreciate good health
After our bodies are racked with pain.

At times we travel to distant places
To satisfy an inner urge to roam;
But then at the end of each of our journeys
We find there's no place quite like home.

Someone slights us or treats us rudely
And in our hurt we try to defend;

Then through the tensions of our misunderstandings
Glows the warm smile of a cherished friend.

When that last cool evening approaches,
And our sun sinks from the skies above,
We make our way toward our Eternal Home
And are enfolded with God's Heavenly Love.

Understanding

Are you having any problems with anyone else? Do you find it difficult to keep your "cool" when you are with certain people? Most of us experience these feelings in some of our relationships, maybe in the business, church, civic, neighborhood, or, too often, family setting. It is not the place that causes most of these problems, it is the people involved.

I have found it beneficial to try to determine the reason why I feel as I do in these cases. I cannot know how the other person feels, but if I can understand why they act the way they do and why I feel the way I do about it, I can cope with the situation better.

Three years ago a lady who worked at the Air Force Base in Jacksonville, Arkansas, enrolled in one of our motivational workshops. Between the first and second meetings, one week apart, the participants were requested to treat everyone with whom they came in contact as the most important person on earth; and if they were having trouble with anyone to get with that person during the week and try to understand the reason for the strained relationship.

This lady returned the second week so excited she could hardly wait for the session to begin so she could report what had happened to her.

She told us that as she was driving home from the first meeting, she chose a woman in her office whom she did not like. She said that she had worked with this woman for over three years and "had never liked her." She continued that she had taken this woman out for a cup of coffee, and during their brief time together she learned that this woman's husband was dying of cancer and that her son was on drugs. There was a shocked silence in our group before the lady continued, "We may never be good friends, but we are going to get along."

As she returned to her seat, I renewed my determination to try to understand others and myself better. Who knows what burdens others may be bearing?

You do not have to enroll in a seminar or read books to seek and find new, happier relationships. Just go out into the mainstream and treat others the way you would want them to treat you and try to understand why others act as they do. Where have we heard this rule before?

A truck driver was driving up a hill in Georgia with a load of live chickens. He was leaning out the window and beating a steel bar on the side of the cab with his left arm. Not believing his eyes, a state trooper flipped on his lights, touched his siren, and motioned the driver to the side of the road. The man parked his truck and walked back to the trooper's car.

"Son," said the trooper, "I hate to tell you, but I'm going to have to take you in for being drunk."

"Just a minute, officer," protested the young truck driver, "I'm not drunk. I haven't even had a drink."

"Don't argue with me. No one acts that way who hasn't been drinking."

"Officer, you just don't understand my problem."

"What is your problem?"

"I'll tell you. That's a one-ton truck over there and I've got two tons of chickens on the bed; and if I don't keep half of them up in the air all the time, I'll never make it up this hill."

We may not agree with this method of transporting chickens, but we can't arrest the driver for being drunk.

Let us try to understand others, and let us make every effort to be understood. This will eliminate unnecessary conflicts. Again, I do not suggest that you agree with other people's point of view, unless you do; just try to understand why they feel and act the way they do.

It has been said many different ways, but I believe this is my favorite: Never criticize a brave until you have walked a mile in his moccasins.

Love

When we share in the workshops I use a chalkboard upon which I write all the suggestions made by the group in response to my question of what we can do to be bigger and better people—to fly a little higher. Many great ideas are shared, sometimes as many as thirty or forty.

In most adult classes, we get answers of honesty, positive thinking, patience, prayer, goals, helpfulness, respect, and many more, all of which, if practiced, would make us better people. However, there is one which, for some reason, older adult classes are reluctant to suggest, while teenagers and young people nearly always suggest it early in the discussion. I let the cat out of the bag by putting it at the beginning of this section. Why do young people say "love" while we adults are reluctant to mention it? I do not know, but it happens so frequently there has to be a reason. It is such a simple-sounding thing, yet if we would just practice it as we should, we and those with whom we come in contact would be happier and better and would fly a little higher.

Earl Nightingale says that we need to love a little more and hate a little less. If we have a thousand friends, we do not have too many friends; but if we have one enemy we have way too many enemies.

In 1972 Bill Gove spoke to a Human Resources Congress in Chicago. The audience numbered about seven hundred, gathered from the United States and several foreign countries. He gave all of us inspirational food for thought, including these two ideas.

Bill Gove said rather simply, but very forcefully, "Ladies and gentlemen, you need to start a love affair with yourselves." He went on to say that we should not go around patting ourselves on the back and declaring that we are the greatest. Oh, no; he said that we should say to ourselves that with all our faults and blunders, peculiarities and shortcomings, God has given each of us a great potential and that it is this potential that we should learn to love and to respect and to develop.

If I really do not like myself there is very little chance that I can ever like you. The second greatest commandment is not "Love thy neighbor." Not at all. The second greatest commandment is "Love thy neighbor as thyself."

Then this speaker really shook us up when he asked if we loved our children or used our children. I immediately thought of our two daughters and our grandchildren. You grandparents know that special relationship that exists between you and your grandchildren. You have to experience it to appreciate it fully.

A friend of mine was waiting at the air terminal to catch his plane, which was running about forty-five minutes late. An acquaintance of his came over and with great pride asked, "John, have I told you about my new grandson?"

"No, and I really appreciate it," came the deflating reply.

To illustrate the point he was making, our speaker told the story of a father who turned to his seventeen-year-old son and laid down the law. He told his son in no uncertain terms that unless he got his long hair cut he would not get to use the family car another time. Bill Gove said very carefully that this father might be saying to his son that he wanted him to look bad in his peer group so that he, the father, could look good in *his* peer group. Perhaps this father wanted to go down to his club and say to his friends gathered there, "My boy doesn't go around with his hair hanging down to his shoulders."

This would make him look pretty important, wouldn't it? But at home there would be a fast-growing seventeen-year-old adolescent, self-conscious and trying to fight his way from boyhood into manhood, who might have had to go back to his group and face embarrassment or even ostracism because he no longer looked like one of them. Who among us likes embarrassment or rejection?

Then this speaker set the record straight. He told us that if this father insists upon his son's doing something for the son's benefit—this being the sole motivation—then regardless of the emotional sparks generated at the time, patience and love and understanding would heal the wound. If, on the other hand, that father, or one of us, asks someone else to do something solely for our own benefit, someone else might be injured for life. We operate at the feeling level, not the intellectual level.

Please answer this question in your mind. If you had to make a choice at this very moment between a physical injury or a severe emotional injury, which would you choose? You might be interested to know that literally thousands of people have been asked this question and not a single one has chosen the emotional injury. Most of us have been physically hurt once or more and in most cases these injuries have healed without any serious after-effects. Most of us have been emotionally hurt, and when those unhappy experiences come to mind, we may feel the pain and anguish that came to us at the time. Many emotional injuries never heal.

When I was in the service during World War II I served with a man from Cleveland, Ohio. He was one of those unfortunate individuals who upon hearing of an illness, reading about a disease, or meeting someone under the weather becomes sick himself. This friend went into open field drills with every pocket filled to overflowing with tonics, pills, and salves. Believe it or not, he did not have the most serious problem in his family. His wife did.

When she was a little girl she stepped into a henhouse and frightened the chickens, which flew up in her face. The effects of this harrowing experience have haunted this lady all her life. As an adult, if she eats anything with eggs in it or sits close to anyone wearing feathers, she breaks out in a serious rash. I am not speaking of prickly heat; I am speaking of large welts all over her body. Ask this lady which she would choose—tripping as she entered that henhouse and breaking her arm or suffering all these years from the emotional injury—and you know what her answer would be. We operate at the feeling level, and we must constantly be on guard against saying anything or doing anything that might injure another person for life.

Many of my friends ask me why I went to law school, earned an LL.B. degree, yet do not practice law. The answer is very simple to me even though I am sure that others do not fully understand. You see, I am a very empathetic person. If I am near an individual either in person or in thought, I can feel his pain and when he hurts I hurt with him.

Anna Mae and I have gone overseas four times on the singing missions I mentioned earlier, visiting several European and Scandinavian countries. We have sung in churches, cathedrals, and military installations, on airplanes and on boats—just about anywhere we found people to listen. In 1978 we visited the Bridge of Sighs in Italy and the dungeon where Paul was held. As we looked around, I began to suffer such severe emotional and physical pain that I was forced to leave my group and walk away.

Therefore, I will not read a book on violence unless it is required reading; I will not view a picture show or television program on violence unless it is required viewing; and I will not remain in a situation where violence is occurring unless I can be of service, because of the emotional impact it has on me. Since my law practice involved many emotional situations over which I had little or no control, I decided to let my brother Jim do the legal work, and I would go out and share ideas with others on how we can live more meaningful, happy lives.

I shall never forget a motion picture I saw several years ago. If you saw it I feel sure that you will remember it also. It was entitled *Where the Lilies Bloom*. The story revolves around a motherless family in Appalachia. The father is close to death from what they called "consumption"—most probably tuberculosis. There were three beautiful children—a girl in her late teens, a second girl about thirteen, and a little boy about nine.

As the father lies on his deathbed, he calls the thirteen-year-old to his bedside and exacts two promises from her. First, she is not to tell anyone outside the family that he has died lest the children be split up, for he wants them to stay together; and second, she is to do everything to prevent her older sister from marrying a certain boy down the valley who is "no good for her."

The father dies, and as promised, the little girl takes over. The children walk the sloping hillsides gathering berries and leaves and digging roots to sell to companies for medicinal purposes.

Almost every day the boy down the valley comes over to talk to the "paw." The younger daughter puts him off again and again and again. Finally, the boy realizes that the father is no longer part of this earthly plane, even though she never tells him. He brings food the family desperately needs. He loans them a little four-wheel vehicle that, as I recall, they wreck. When the younger girl realizes that the boy down the valley is an okay kind of fellow, she gives her sister permission to marry him although she knows at that very moment she is breaking one of the promises she made to her father on his death-bed.

Then came that unforgettable, moving final scene. This courageous little girl, with a hand-sewn dress upon her body, stands all alone on the sloping hillside. The mists of the valley gently caress her shoulders. Looking down at her father's grave, covered with native stones, she speaks softly and apologetically, "Paw, you were wrong about ole Joe, but you can still love someone even though they are wrong."

I have heard our daughter say to her daughter, "Helen, I love you, but I don't love what you did."

After all these years of knowing that God is love, I now realize how limited my concept has been. I know that we are channels of this great flow of universal energy and our responsibility is to let it flow unimpeded by hate, jealousy, envy, or resentment. In this way we can see that we have the potential of loving everyone.

So, indeed, you and I need to love a little more and hate a little less.

If you feel that you have an enemy, someone who stirs

strong feelings of hate, resentment, or jealousy within you when he comes to mind, I would like to suggest one possibility to help you rid yourself of his control over your life. This suggestion has worked for several people.

The next time this person comes to mind and you begin to feel angry and your blood pressure begins to rise, find a quiet place where you can be alone. Then take out a pen or pencil and some paper and make a list of everything you would like to say to that person. You might even begin by writing, "I hate you because—" Write down everything you can think of that makes you feel as you do about this person. Seal the paper in an envelope and hide it where only you can find it. Let your anger be sealed in the envelope.

The next time this person comes to mind and you get that old feeling, go back, open the envelope, read what you have written, and add any more things you have thought of since the last time. Seal it again and put it away.

If you persist, the day will come when you will open that envelope, read what you have written, and get a little embarrassed about the way you have felt. You might find yourself uttering a little silent prayer that your feelings were sealed in an envelope and not spoken to that person.

When the tensions begin to ease and your anger no longer possesses you, the logjam will begin to break up, and you will be on your way back up. It is not easy, but isn't it worth a try? Who knows, "that person" might become a good friend once the misunderstandings are removed.

Dear friend, I accept you for what you are,
Not for what I wish you to be,
And I hope that in this spirit of love—
Though imperfect—you will accept me.

I am not satisfied with my life,
But I will strive each day
To lift a load—to right a wrong—
As I travel along life's way.

I will strive to see the good
In what men say and do,
For when I love as I should love,
Gray skies will turn to blue.

I want to be God's channel of love
And let it freely flow
Through me to everyone I meet
On this earth here below.

For I know that in that place
Christ has prepared for us above,
That you and I will be engulfed
In God's universal love.

Enthusiasm

Many articles have been written, seminars conducted, speeches made, sermons preached, and personal experiences shared on the most contagious of our human emotions—enthusiasm. Love is the strongest and most beneficial emotion, but enthusiasm is the most contagious.

Every machine ever invented and constructed by man must have a source of energy or it will not operate. Every person, even those with great potential, will remain mediocre without enthusiasm. It is the "go juice" in human relations.

A friend of mine who worked for a frozen food company was called on the carpet by his boss. It seems that the trucks were not getting away on time. In these days when you seldom hear "What's cooking?" but rather "What's thawing?" this created a very serious problem.

My friend at first did what I find myself doing when something goes wrong. He sought an outside cause for his problem.

He told his boss that they should redesign the loading dock so that the trucks could be loaded differently. Ten thousand dollars was spent, and according to Bill it didn't help one bit. Now Bill's job was in jeopardy. He decided to try enthusiasm. He did not tell his fellow workers. He did not put a notice on the bulletin board. He just decided to get excited about his job and the opportunities he faced. His excitement spread, as it most often does, and later Bill told me what had happened. He said they were loading the same trucks, with the same crews, putting on more merchandise, and spending only two-thirds of the time previously required to get the job done. This is a wonderful example of the magic of enthusiasm.

Often when I am to make a talk, someone who has heard me before asks me to be sure to tell the train story. Perhaps you will enjoy the train story as well.

Three men were seated in a diner eating a snack, when one of them looked at his watch and exclaimed, "Oh, my goodness, that train is leaving."

They jumped up, paid their bills, and rushed pell-mell across the street and up the steps to the train level. The long-legged fellow led the way, taking two and three steps at a time. The next man wasn't too far behind, but the third little fat fellow, with a bag in his hand, was a distant third.

When the first man reached the train level, the train had begun to move. He leaped on the observation car, caught the second man by the wrists, and pulled him aboard. Then the two of them shouted encouragement to the little fat man who was just coming into view at the top of the steps. He did his best, but his best wasn't good enough. Dropping his bags, he wiped the sweat off his brow just as the trainman ran up.

"Gee, I'm sure sorry you missed your train," consoled the trainman.

"That ain't the half of it," said the traveler, trying to catch his breath.

"What do you mean by that?" inquired the trainman.

"Do you see them two fellows waving at me from the observation car?" asked the bewildered little fat man.

"Of course I see them," replied the trainman.

"They came down here to see me off."

Get excited about the things you do, and if you cannot get excited—if you do not feel challenged by the opportunities you have each day—then perhaps it is time for you to take stock. If, after looking at your situation as objectively as possible, you can find no reasons to get excited and enthusiastic, it might be well for you to consider some options. Perhaps a door is open that you have not seen before—a door that will lead you to a fuller, happier, more productive life.

However, I caution you: our attitudes toward our jobs have a tendency to lose their luster over a long period of time, and what we really need to do is to improve our attitudes, rekindle the fires of enthusiasm, and fly a little higher.

Seated in the office of my friend Stanley Russ in Conway, I heard a truism that I recommend you commit to memory and apply to your life as I try to apply it to mine, and I can assure you that your life will never be the same. It is pure gold. *It is your attitude, not your aptitude, which will determine your altitude.*

My calling card expresses this thought in a verse written several years ago:

All men must choose
The way they'll go—
To reach their secret dream.
In spite of storms
That threaten them—
Unafraid of the rising stream—
Dedicated to nobler things—
Enthusiastic to the end—
Save a place at the top—I say
  Good ATTITUDES always win!

"Laughter Is the Hand of God"

She walked up to me after our meeting was over and said, "Mr. Gannaway, I didn't want to come tonight; my husband made me come. My twin sons have just joined the Marines and I have been in tears all day long. But," she continued, "this seminar was just for me and I really appreciate it." She turned to leave and then, pausing, she asked, "Have you heard this one: 'Laughter is the hand of God on the shoulder of a troubled world'?"

How true it is.

Any time or any place I am given the opportunity to speak, I try to begin by affirming, *This is the day the Lord has made. Let us rejoice and be glad in it.* Then I begin to fulfill one of my missions—to get my listeners to laugh. I believe that a good, hearty laugh is essential to successful everyday living. As a matter of fact, I am so convinced that laughter is critical to each of us that I want to issue a very serious challenge to you. If you go home at the end of any then apply our talents to reach them.

Mr. Nightingale also says that the world will stand aside and let the man pass who knows where he is going.

Have you ever wondered why some people rise to the top, while others with seemingly equal opportunities and like ability never seem to get off the ground?

There are many reasons, but I have found that one major cause is the failure to choose a worthy goal or destination and then the failure to put forth every effort to get there. Just wanting something in life is not enough; we must want that certain something so badly that we are willing to put forth our best efforts until we get it. If a door slams in our faces, we should try the next door and the next and the next, never giving up.

Major disappointments are quite often blessings in disguise if we but have the patience to pause along the way and view our present situation objectively. I have found that everything that happens to me, whether positive or negative, is an opportunity to learn. I am responsible for determining and profiting from the lesson.

When I was in my late teens, I set as my goal to have a career in singing. I learned to play the guitar. I got a letter of introduction to a company in Hollywood and the promise of a six months' contract with CBS in New York City.

That fall before I was to leave home to become a "star," something happened that changed my plans and my life.

My brothers Malcolm and Jim and I were returning from a hunting trip with an older friend of ours. At twilight, that dangerous time of day, we struck a large truck loaded with cotton seeds. I was seated in the front seat on the passenger side. The impact threw me against the steering wheel, severely damaging my throat. We were rushed to a small hospital in a community south of Little Rock. The doctors ministered to us as best they could and gave me twenty minutes to live. Boy, I'm glad they were wrong!

When I began to recover, I could talk, but only in a monotone. My father persuaded a physician he knew from Virginia, his home state, to come to Little Rock to examine me. The verdict: "He will never sing again and will probably have to speak in a monotone the rest of his life." My dreams were shattered and my hopes destroyed in one brief moment, but I was still alive.

I attended law school and began a career in the legal profession with my father.

Then came that wonderful, unforgettable Sunday when I walked about a foot off the carpeted aisle, processing with our choir to sing again.

I have a cousin in the entertainment field who does an outstanding job, and it took a near-fatal accident to keep me from trying to follow in his footsteps.

Now I realize that what was a major disappointment at that time was really a blessing. I never would have been happy in a full-time singing career. Oh, to be sure, I sing a lot—church choir, overseas singing missions, programs for groups, and just singing to myself as I drive along the highway alone. A door was slammed in my face, but I found an open door that led me to what I now do, and I am happy sharing ideas with others.

You may be saying, "Bob, I agree with you and I want to do something really worthwhile with my life, but how do I go about it?" Understanding a few basic facts about the conscious and the subconscious mind will help.

The Human Mind

According to the experts, the human mind is divided into two parts, the conscious and the subconscious. The conscious mind is the reasoning mind; the subconscious mind neither reasons nor knows right from wrong, good

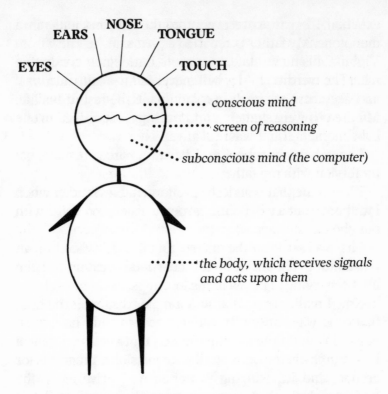

EYES EARS NOSE TONGUE TOUCH

.... conscious mind
..·········screen of reasoning
····· subconscious mind (the computer)

···········the body, which receives signals
and acts upon them

**(If this little stick figure reminds you
of someone you know, it is purely
coincidental.)**

from bad. The conscious mind rests; the subconscious mind never rests.

Between the conscious and subconscious minds is the screen of reasoning. We consider something and either accept or reject it at the screen of reasoning. If is it accepted, the thought is recorded in the subconscious mind for immediate action or filed away for future reference. The experts tell us that everything that ever happens to us that is not rejected at the screen of reasoning is filed in the subconscious. This is the reason some experts believe that at age seventy the subconscious mind may store as many as three trillion items.

You may know that experiments are being conducted where an unborn child is being exposed to beautiful music and literature, with the probability that its life will be affected by messages and feelings recorded in its subconscious mind before physical birth.

The subconscious is the computer. We are responsible for the way it is programmed by our thinking.

When you picked up this book to read, your conscious mind entertained the idea; your thought passed through the screen of reasoning; the subconscious received the signals and sent the impulse to your hand, which in turn picked up the book. Suppose you start to pick up a snake. This thought reaches your screen of reasoning, and you decide whether to accept or reject this suggestion. Many people handle snakes for different reasons; however, most of us give them plenty of room. So most of us reject this idea, no signal is sent to the subconscious, and our hands do not pick up the snake.

The information we are to consider and either accept or reject is collected by the five antennae of sight, sound, taste, smell and touch.

For example, I do not know your name, in most cases, but you know mine. Why do I not know your name? I have never had the pleasure of meeting you. You know my name because it is written on the face of this book. This information that you have, and the fact that I do not have the same information about you, has nothing to do with our respective intelligence. It is only that you have been exposed to my name by sight and perhaps sound, and I have neither heard nor read your name.

I usually show my audiences a piece of chalk and ask them to identify it. Of course, they all know what a piece of chalk looks like, but they also know that it makes a noise as it touches the chalkboard; it has a certain feeling when we hold it; and it even has a slight odor and a chalky taste. So all five senses are involved with a piece of chalk.

Suppose, however, we take that same piece of chalk and show it to one of the tribes of Africa or South America and ask them, through an interpreter, to identify it. Do you suppose they would know what it is? Probably not. If, on the other hand, they were familiar with something that looked like a piece of chalk, they would probably tell us that it was the object with which they were familiar. Our subconscious knows the chalk; their subconscious knows another item that looks like chalk.

Then I show the group a buckeye. Many know what it is immediately, but a large percentage have never seen a buckeye and are baffled. When they are told what it is, I usually let some of them hold it. Now they have seen it, heard it identified, and felt it. Into their subconscious goes this information, and the next time they see a buckeye they will know what it is.

You may hear a familiar strain of music and suddenly recall that this is the music the band played at your senior prom. You begin to picture other people who were there. You may recall your date, whom you may not have thought of in years. The feeling of joy or disgust you experienced that night will also return—for the emotions experienced with each event are filed with your memory of that particular event.

A young man with a disappointing blind date sat over in the corner during a band break. She talked romance and he talked weather. She talked romance and he tried politics. Finally, in desperation, he walked over to the refreshment table and returned with two cups of punch. She took her cup and, leaning over close to him, whispered, "If you can guess what I hold in my hand, I'll let you kiss me."

He looked at her tightly clenched fist and with a feeling of relief said, "It's an elephant."

"Close enough!" she squealed.

She had set her goal and would not be denied.

Perhaps one day as you are walking down your street on a crisp November day, you will smell the rich aroma of a turkey being roasted for Thanksgiving. Your mind may furnish you with pictures of those times you went to your grandmother's for that special day. In all probability, you will not see a large brown bird on a platter. You most probably will see the faces and hear the voices of aunts and uncles and cousins you haven't seen or thought about for years. It is all recorded in your subconscious mind waiting to be triggered by some event that brings the experience into sharp focus.

I related this example to a group one night at an insurance company meeting and as I said "grandmother" I happened to be looking to my right. As I spoke this one word, a lady suddenly burst into tears. There was no sound—just large tears rolling down her cheeks.

I missed her after the meeting that evening so the next day I went to her office to talk with her. I explained that I had noticed her response to my mention of a grandmother. She sat for a moment and then said to me, "Yes, I was raised by my grandmother, and I loved her so much that when she died a part of me died with her."

Her love for her grandmother and her deep feeling of loss triggered her reaction. The emotion attached to her experiences with her grandmother returned with the thought.

Speaking of Thanksgiving, I smile every time I think of the story of a little girl watching her mother prepare the Thanksgiving turkey. Her mother picked up a large knife, chopped the tail off the turkey, placed it in the pan, and slid it into the oven.

"Mommy, mommy," exclaimed the girl in an excited voice, "why did you chop the tail off the turkey?"

Her mother thought for a moment and then replied, "Honey, I really don't know. My mother always did it."

The little girl had to have an answer, so she went to her grandmother. But her grandmother did not know either. She just did it because she had seen her mother do it that way.Fortunately, the great-grandmother was still alive, and here the little girl found her answer.

"You see, dear, when we were raising our family, we didn't have enough money to buy a large pan, so I had to cut the tail off the turkey to get it into the pan."

Three generations chopping the tail off the turkey, and only one of the three had a valid reason for doing it. What a pity! If you and I are not careful, we will find ourselves caught up in conformity and will spend needless time and energy doing things for no rhyme or reason, just because someone else did it that way.

A man was suffering from a severe earache. He walked into a strange doctor's office seeking relief. The receptionist gathered the necessary information of his name, address, telephone number, and symptoms. Then she told him to go into the room at the end of the hall, where he would find some hospital gowns. He was to remove all his clothes, don a hospital gown, and wait to be seen.

He stood for a moment in shocked silence and then protested, "Nurse, I believe you misunderstood me. It is my ear that is bothering me, so I do not believe it will be necessary for me to put on a hospital gown."

He was dumbfounded by her next remarks. "We have a procedure we always follow in this office. Every patient that my doctor sees must have on a hospital gown. So if you want him to see you, you must put on a hospital gown."

Not wanting to seek another doctor, he retreated to the

room and began to disrobe. Glancing up, he saw a man who had arrived before him and was standing in the corner, a little embarrassed, with his hospital gown pulled around him.

"This is the craziest place I have ever seen," exclaimed the man as he continued to disrobe. "I came in here with an earache and they told me I'd have to put on this hospital gown before the doctor would see me."

"Shucks, fellow, what are you fussin' about?" said the other. "I came in here to fix his telephone."

Conformity, that old, deadly adversary, was at work. We find it in all areas of our daily lives. What a waste of time and energy! If a procedure is productive, of course, it should be followed, but if not, then we should seek a better way—and there is always a better way if we are wise enough to find it.

Our subconscious minds are programmed in three ways. The first way is by repetition. Phone numbers, home or business addresses, and simple arithmetic are unemotional bits of information, which may be impressed upon the subconscious merely by rote.

The second way the subconscious mind is programmed is by a traumatic experience, something that shocks the nervous system and requires no repetition—either joy or sorrow, so long as the emotions are involved.

To illustrate this point I ask seminar participants to raise their hands if they remember where they were and what they were doing when they learned that President John F. Kennedy had been assassinated. Nearly all who were old enough to comprehend it at that time raise their hands. When given the time, they can recall the most minute details of that moment, such as what they were wearing, others who were present, and their immediate reaction. I myself remember those details very vividly.

Then I ask for a show of hands of those who remember

what they were doing and where they were when they learned of the death of President Harry S. Truman. Occasionally someone will raise his hand—a cousin or someone who was close to President Truman. Most of us, though, do not remember the exact moment when we learned of his passing. Why not? They were both great presidents in their own right and they are both dead. The reason is obvious. President Kennedy's life was snuffed out by an assassin's bullet while President Truman died quietly and peacefully. Our subconscious minds are impressed by emotional experiences.

Would you believe that a man in my Ravenna, Ohio, class said he didn't know that Harry Truman had died?

Remember that the subconscious mind does not know right from wrong. It cannot distinguish what is good or bad for us. Like a computer, it accepts unquestioningly the thoughts we let pass through our screen of reasoning.

It behooves each of us to consider carefully the programs we allow to pass into our subconscious minds. We must have a dream if we expect a dream to come true, but dreams may become nightmares.

There was a time in the not-too-distant past when some of the patients in our mental institutions were kept in what were known as violent wards. In many cases chains were used to restrain them.

One day a visitor was being shown through one of these wards. When he and the guard passed a cell he observed a patient straining at his chains and mumbling, "Mary, Mary, Mary."

"What happened to him?" asked the visitor.

"Oh, he was engaged to a girl named Mary and she jilted him," was the reply. "It just tipped him off the deep end."

In a few minutes they approached another cell in which the inmate was behaving in a similar manner, only more violently.

"Mary, Mary, Mary," he groaned, rattling his chains.

"Well, what happened to him?" inquired the puzzled visitor.

"Oh," came the reply. "He married her."

We must be sure that we really want the things we think we want, because we are most likely to get them; and then we may find out we didn't want them at all.

We were invited to a home one evening to tell a family about some motivational tapes that they might purchase for family use. After completing the interview, we walked to the front door, and the mother of four children said that she had "lived in this house one full year before we ever started building it."

She had pictured in her mind the arrangement of the rooms and the placement of windows and doors. These pictures passed through her screen of reasoning, and a strong program was put into her subconscious. The signal was continually strengthened as she collected pictures, visited other homes, and talked with builders and contractors. Signals were sent to her body, and actual construction began on the home she had dreamed of for a full year. Now she lives in it.

Have you ever told your children that they are dumb, stupid, ugly, mean, or any other such negative thing? Be careful. If they are not able to reject your program, but let it pass through their screen of reasoning into their conputer—their subconscious mind—you may find them acting that way.

I try to play tennis three times a week from 6:30 to around 8:00 a.m. We usually play doubles. When one of the regulars is unable to play, we invite someone else to fill in. One of the men we invite occasionally is a good tennis player, but he is hard on himself. Whenever he makes a poor shot, you can hear him say something like, "Look at the ball, stupid; bend your knees, stupid," and after a few games I believe that I can see his game going down.

Doing a stupid act (I certainly do my share of them) is not the same thing as being stupid.

The third way the subconscious mind is programmed is by hypnosis. As we sit in the comfort of our own living room or den in a favorite chair, without moving or changing our environment, a hypnotist can change our physical comfort dramatically. He removes our reasoning, conscious mind, goes below the screen of reasoning directly to the subconscious mind, and programs it so that it will send false signals to the body.

He can suggest that we are in the Sahara Desert with a temperature of 130 degrees in the shade, and no shade. What does our body immediately do? It begins to perspire profusely. We struggle for breath and may disrobe to the point of modesty in a vain attempt to escape the searing heat. Then he can suggest that we are in Siberia where the temperature is 30 degrees below zero, and the subconscious sends this signal to the body. The body responds and begins to shiver; the teeth chatter and we cannot find enough clothes to fight the bitter cold. In fact, we are neither too hot nor too cold. The subconscious mind does not know this and so it accepts the false information and sends signals to the body, and the body reacts in accordance with the signals. Now, you can see the great danger we face in wrong thinking. We must try at all times to think positive thoughts. We must set worthy goals and reject any suggestion that would create unhappiness, frustration, or tension.

A young salesman was being trained by a manager with many years of experience. As they drove along the street the sales manager told the young salesman to pull into the parking lot of a business establishment so they could sell them some merchandise.

"They won't buy anything," protested the young salesman.

"Stop this car," ordered the older man. "Young man," he lectured, "if you ever expect to be a successful salesman you have to be positive."

"Okay, sir," complied the young trainee, "I'm positive they won't buy anything."

This is what is known as positive negative.

Now that we understand how our minds work, it is time to roll up our sleeves and go to work. Regardless of what you have been told or what you may have told yourself, it does not have to be that way unless you allow the signals to reach your subconscious mind. Learn to reject negative, defeating thoughts. Think of the bumblebee and take off on a journey to new places, and experience the joy that comes from accomplishments.

How many times did the great Thomas Edison try and fail, only to try again and again, before he finally succeeded in perfecting a method to control electric light? What an inspiration! With every dream must come labor, if we are to be successful in making our dreams come true. Desire is essential to any undertaking, but desire without work is useless.

A distraught housewife went to a marriage counselor for help. Tearfully she related that every morning her husband threw back the covers, went and opened the window, and then spent thirty or forty minutes exercising. He would then proceed to the bathroom, where he showered and shaved, all the time singing to himself. Returning to the bedroom, smelling of expensive aftershave lotion, he would put on one of his $500 suits with matching necktie. Then he would go down to eat a nutritious, healthful breakfast. After breakfast he would stand in front of the mirror, look himself in the eye, and, straightening his necktie, proclaim, "You are the greatest. You can do anything you want to do."

"Lady," interrupted the counselor, "I believe you have come to the wrong place. This is one of the most wonderful stories I have ever heard. What is the problem?"

"He never leaves home," was the reply.

Dressing well, exercising, eating proper food, and holding positive thoughts about oneself are all good, but they are of little value unless we walk out the door, enter the marketplace, and go to work to make our dreams come true by making things happen.

Some of us have a tendency to reach a goal and then rest on our laurels. When a goal has been reached, we should set another goal—of something else we want to do, some other place where we want to go. That is why so many retired people die a few years after retirement. They have nothing to do, no dream—nothing to challenge them and give them an exciting reason to get out of bed and make things happen.

When I was about ten years old, my mother took me to hear the great Metropolitan tenor Richard Crooks in a live performance in Little Rock. After the recital Mother took me up on the stage to meet him.

I said, "Mr. Crooks, I really enjoyed your singing this evening."

He looked down at me with a warm smile and said something I shall never forget.

"Young man, I appreciate what you have said, but my performance in Little Rock tonight will not do me any good tomorrow night in Memphis. I've got to be good tomorrow night in Memphis."

This makes good sense. We must keep moving forward and upward, not resting on past accomplishments, or we may forget how to fly.

Lord, give me a mission in this life,
One you would have me fulfill,
Whether it be up the dusty Palestinean roads
Or the path up Calvary's hill.

Point my steps to places of need
And tune my ear to the cries of the lonely.
Let me reach out to lift the fallen
And think of others' needs only.

Keep me from complaining when the load is heavy
And dark clouds cover the sun.
May I rise up when I stumble
That life's race I may continue to run.

Then when the sun begins to set
And I am no longer able to roam,
Lord, let me hear you say, "Well done,
Faithful servant, it's time to come home."

What Bugs You?

As you read these lines, is anything bothering you? Have you spent any time and energy today worrying about something or someone? If you haven't, you are in a class all by yourself.

A well-known doctor has stated that over half of all hospital beds are occupied by patients who, whether they are suffering from high blood pressure, stomach ulcers, heart problems, or a nervous breakdown, are all hospitalized as a result of worry.

Let us see if we can put our worries in their proper place. I do not offer a money-back guarantee that you will get rid of your worries, but only that when you learn to put them in their proper perspective you will find them more manageable.

Abraham Lincoln is reputed to have said, "If you can't make a mistake, you can't make anything."

This certainly is true, and his statement provides us

with a good starting place. Anyone who does anything is going to make mistakes. The biggest mistake one can make is not to do anything.

I have a sign in my office that reads, "You can't change yesterday, but you can ruin today by worrying about tomorrow." Something to think about.

A friend of mine quipped, "Worries are like a rocking chair. They will give you something to do, but they won't get you anyplace." True logic.

One of our granddaughters, Mary Jane, aged ten, is what I like to describe as "plugged into the universe." I know of no other way to explain her words of wisdom. When she was about three, she walked down a hallway closing doors on either side and leaving the door at the end of the hall open. Then, turning to her mother, she said that death was like that—a dark tunnel and a bright light at the end. If you have read any of the recent studies on life after death, you know that this is the way those who have died clinically and returned describe their experiences—as a walk through darkness and then an emergence into dazzling, brilliant light.

When Mary Jane was five, she said to her mother, "If you haven't forgotten yesterday, yesterday becomes today." What words of wisdom!

After meditating on these words for a while, I believe I know what Mary Jane was saying. Since our minds can hold only one thought at a time, if our thought is of yesterday, then we bring that thought into today and we are living in the past. Wish I could say things like that.

Quite often we dwell in the past, wishing we could do it all over again and change things, but we can't. So we must think about today—right now—for this is the only time we have to use—the immediate present.

Many people, through trial and error, discover ways to relax and relieve tensions. Another sign in my office reads, "I'm so used to being tense that when I relax I get nervous." We know a certain amount of tension is productive. It helps us to reach our goals, but we must try to control our tensions and not allow them to control us. Sometimes we need to blow off a little steam. Some people beat on a pillow and scream; some take strenuous physical exercise; others may withdraw for a time of quiet meditation.

When I was in west Texas working with the school districts there, I heard a wonderful story of how one American boy blew off steam. This little boy's family had moved to Mexico for an extended period of time, and he was enrolled in an English-speaking, Mexican-operated school. About the second or third day, the teacher was inquiring about American history.

"What American president said, 'Ask not what your country can do for you, but what you can do for your country'?" she queried.

The American boy raised his hand, but the teacher called on a Mexican child who identified the president as John F. Kennedy.

"Very good," said the teacher. "Now, who said, 'The only thing we have to fear is fear itself'?"

Again the American boy raised his hand, only to be ignored as another Mexican child answered that this was President Franklin D. Roosevelt. Every time a question was asked the American boy waved his hand frantically, hoping to be called on so he could make a good grade, but he was ignored. Pressure began to build and he got madder and madder. When the teacher completed this part of the lesson and turned to write something on the chalkboard, the boy exploded: "I hate these blankety-blank Mexicans."

Spinning around, the teacher demanded, "Who said that?"

"Davy Crockett at the Alamo," was the quick reply.

Maybe he did not receive a good grade for his answer, but he is bound to have felt better after letting off a little steam.

Whenever I am introduced as an expert, I quickly give my listeners my definition of an expert so as to relieve any pressure that might be placed on me by the audience's expecting too much. I agree that I am an expert in the field of motivation only if they accept my definition of an expert. *An expert is an individual who speaks to you in a confused manner about a subject he little understands, but he explains it in such a way that he makes you think the confusion is all your fault.*

Again we call upon experts' information to help us place our worries in their proper perspective.

Experts tell us that 40 percent of our worries never happen. How about that? We have just started, and we can eliminate almost half of our worries because they never happen.

At a healing workshop in St. Louis, a speaker who had studied world religions told us of the Zen religion. As I recall his presentation, he said that a young person might spend as long as several years in mental, physical, emotional, and spiritual training to become a Zen master.

He told of an old master who called his protégé to his side and told him of a problem that needed to be solved. He said that someone had slipped a goose egg through the mouth of a large, valuable, ancient glass jug and controlled the temperature and humidity so that the egg hatched. The little gosling was fed and watered until it grew to fill the jug completely. Now the problem: how could they get the goose out of the jug without breaking the jug? The young man left. For three days and nights he struggled with the problem. He did the mental, physical, and spiritual exercises he had been taught. He prayed without success. Finally, completely defeated, he returned to his master and said, "I have failed you. I cannot get the goose out of the jug, and I need your help."

The wise old master replied simply, "Bring me the jug."

But there was no jug, there was no egg, there was no goose, and there was no problem. The young man had spent three frustrating days and nights in vain. The experts tell us that we spend 40 percent of our time trying to get geese out of jugs that do not exist in the first place.

Furthermore, we spend 30 percent of our time worrying about things that have already happened and are over and done with. As one husband suggested to his wife, "Honey, don't trip over something right behind you." Good advice for all of us.

Don't waste valuable time and energy worrying about things that have already happened. Look ahead to opportunities coming your way—though I suggest this with a casual warning: if everything seems to be coming your way, you may be in the wrong lane.

A little boy ran into the kitchen and announced excitedly, "Mommy, mommy, there's a big black bear out in the neighbor's backyard."

"No way, son," she answered reassuringly.

"Yes, there is, Mommy. Come and see."

The mother walked with her son onto the back porch and saw a large black dog running around. In order to teach her son a lesson she reprimanded, "That's not a bear; that's a dog. We are not going to have story-telling in this house. You go upstairs and ask God to forgive you for telling a story."

The little boy did as he was told, and the mother went back to her chores. In a few minutes she heard him bounding down the steps. She asked him if he had asked God to forgive him.

"Yes, Mommy, I asked God to forgive me, and He did."

"How do you know God forgave you?"

"He told me not to worry about it. He said the first time He saw it He thought it was a bear too."

The animal had been a bear or a dog from its conception, and no amount of worry could change that. Yet we spend 30 percent of our time worrying about things that have already happened.

We all know of people who have made themselves deathly ill by negative thinking, and we know of those who have baffled medical science by their "unexplained" recoveries when the doctors had given up hope of a recovery.

My good friend Harold Sherman, researcher, lecturer, and author in the field of the powers of the human mind, tells me of two older lady friends of his. One of these is so negative that Harold says he would walk around the block to avoid seeing her. Whenever they meet he says he gets "an organ recital." Her stomach, liver, gall bladder, or something is bothering her every time.

The other friend is just the opposite. Crippling arthritis has restricted her to a wheelchair, but she is always cheerful and enthusiastic about everyday living. One day Harold told her how much he admired her and appreciated her ability to smile through her obvious pain and spread sunshine on those who came to see her. Her reply should be chiseled in stone for all generations to read: "Mr. Sherman, I never let my body talk back to me."

Shame on us of healthy bodies and minds for our complaining.

Twelve percent of our time is spent in needless worries about our health. Notice the word "needless."

In about 1960, a man in a class in Pine Bluff stood up and said he would like to relate an incident that had occurred several weeks before. He said that he was a little embarrassed to tell it, but that it might help someone else.

One night he was awakened by a severe pain in his side. He reached under the covers and felt a large knot. He was shaken, but decided to ignore it, hoping it would go away. That didn't work, for when he awoke the next morning it was still there and, if anything, had grown a little. He decided to try a different approach. He would not shower but would just dress and go to work without looking. Again—failure. That night when he felt the lump, it had indeed grown and if anything was more tender. He decided he had no other choice except to accept the awful truth. He loosened his belt, turned down his pants, and—that's right; you have probably already guessed—found a big tick. He had spent a sleepless night and nonproductive day in needless worry about his health. We spend 12 percent of our time this way.

Ten percent of our time is spent in petty worries—little things that really should not absorb so much time and energy.

I have a friend who sets aside five minutes every day, by his watch, to spend on petty worries. He pushes everything aside, calls forth these trivial annoyances for a brief session, and then dismisses them until the next day. How I wish I had his self-control and self-discipline! I let them creep in without any control on my part, and soon I find they are requiring time and energy that could be spent more productively in other ways.

When I was a young man my father gave me two books, *Heart Throbs* and *More Heart Throbs*. In one of these there was a poem about a man who read that the sun would burn out in 500 million years. He worried about it. The planets would collide in 300 million years, so he worried about that. All these fantastic things this man worried about, and in the end his wife had to take in washing to make him a living and he didn't worry about that a bit.

It doesn't take a computer to realize that when we spend

40% of our time worrying about things that never happen;

30% worrying about things that have already happened;

12% worrying about our health—needlessly; and

10% worrying about petty things,

this is 92 percent of our time. So out of every hundred things we fret over, only eight are really worthy of our attention. *God, grant me the serenity to accept the things I cannot change, the courage to change those things that I can change, and the wisdom to know the difference.*

If while mowing my lawn I come upon a stick, rock, or piece of wire or paper, I pause, remove the obstacle, and continue my mowing. On the other hand, if I come to that large pine tree in the corner of the yard, I go around it. This is the way we should learn to treat our worries and concerns.

Many people report that they are greatly relieved to know that many other people have worries just as they do and are traveling in the same boat.

Get Off This Bench

Several years ago I read the story of a coach who turned to his fourth-string quarterback and asked him what he would do if his team had the ball on the opponents' 32-yard line, with the score tied and only two minutes left to play. The would-be quarterback thought for a moment and then said excitedly, "Coach, I'll tell you what I would do: I'd move down to the other end of the bench where I could see better."

In my presentations I use this story not as a humorous incident, but as a tragic one. Where does the tragedy lie? Here is a young man training to be a quarterback who in his own thinking cannot project himself onto the playing field, calling the signals and leading the team. Of course, he's not a total loser; he at least thinks to improve his position on the bench. There are days when I doubt that I could do even that. We must be careful not to sit on that proverbial bench mentally, emotionally, or spiritually, lest we never get into the exciting game of life being played before us.

A blinding, driving headache makes us appreciate good health; severe ice and snow storms make us pause to appreciate spring when its flowers burst forth. Bad experiences give us a point of reference for recognizing the good.

When I was an instructor for a speaking course, I became associated with a man named Harold Abbott. Harold suffered a near-fatal heart attack, and I was told he was having a very difficult time adjusting. At one of our meetings I was delighted to see Harold. He seemed to be feeling good again. I told him how glad I was to be with him and to see him doing so well. Then he told me a very inspiring story that had changed his attitude from "Why me?" to "Thank you, Lord."

Harold was attending a company meeting in Chicago. He was standing in front of the hotel window dressing and inwardly complaining about how bad he felt. He looked across the street into the park and observed a beggar, who had a sign around his neck. Everyone who was passing stopped to share with him. Harold had to know what the sign said. He finished dressing and made his way across the street to the beggar. When he got close enough to read the sign, everything in his thinking suddenly went from negative to positive. The sign read, "It's spring and I'm blind."

Have you ever felt that a day was lost—that you had accomplished nothing worthwhile in it? I must admit that I have, many times. Consider this:

A man who had had too much to drink was staggering up the steps to his room, trying not to wake his wife. His unsteady step gave way and he fell, landing on his hip and cutting himself pretty badly on his pocket flask. Pulling himself up, he slipped into the bathroom, removed his clothes, got out the bandaids, and began to patch himself up with the help of the mirror.

The next morning his wife asked innocently, "George, did you come in drunk last night?"

"Honey," he responded, "why in the world would you ask a question like that?"

"Well, only a drunk would put bandaids all over the mirror." This is an example of a nonproductive maneuver!

I am told that in life there is a small group of people that makes things happen. I appreciate the Campus Crusade's definition of the modern-day church: "The modern-day church is like a football game. There are 22 men on the field desperately in need of some rest, and 40,000 in the stands desperately in need of some exercise."

It makes little difference where we go, we always find that within every organization it is a small group that makes things happen.

Most people watch things happen and then move. Braves need chiefs and chiefs need braves, but most of us wait for something to happen before we react.

When I was in the military service I served in the Counterintelligence Corps and was stationed for a while in Dallas, Texas. One night after a meeting at the Baker Hotel we walked into the streets of Dallas, only to find that a fog had locked in the city.

One of the young men leaving the meeting noticed some taillights going in the general direction he wanted to go. He pulled behind the other car and followed it slowly through the streets. After a while it stopped. Its lights went out and the driver came back to my friend's car and demanded, "Young man, why are you following me?"

"Sir," responded my friend, "I apologize if my lights bothered you, but you were going in the general direction

I wanted to go, and I thought I might break out of the fog or recognize my whereabouts."

"Young man," said the other indignantly, "I'm in my garage!"

The great danger we face as followers is that we may find ourselves carrying the wrong flag, marching in the wrong parade, or following the wrong person in the wrong direction. Choices are not always easy, and the paths we choose may be rocky, but we should be responsible for making our own decisions.

Another football story teaches us a valuable lesson: it is not always what we know, but how we apply whatever knowledge we have, that matters. To me this is true wisdom.

A coach had only two quarterbacks. The first-string quarterback was perfection in motion. His play calling was flawless, his leadership was persuasive, and his execution had brought his team to the state championship game. The second-string quarterback came from a different mold. They say that he was so stupid that when he earned his football letter his girlfriend had to read it to him. And he had terrible coordination. The score was tied, the home team was moving down the field, and time was running out. Suddenly a knee injury crumpled the star quarterback. The trainer rushed out, checked the knee, and helped him off the field. He was through for the night.

The coach turned to his second-stringer and told him to get out on the field and finish the game. The substitute jogged onto the field as if he were coming apart at every seam. He looked over the situation, called a play, and advanced to the line. Unbelievably, his play caught the opponents off guard, and the ball carrier scored a winning touchdown.

In the excitement of the dressing room the coach

reached up, grabbed the new star by the shoulder pads, and shouted, "Son, that was just great. How did you know which play to call?"

"Coach, it wasn't easy," came the response.

"I'm sure it wasn't. How did you decide?"

"I'll tell you what I did, Coach. I looked across the line at all them big fellers, and the biggest man I ever seen in a football jersey had a 6 and a 7 on his shirt, so I just added them together and that was 14, so I called 14 and it worked."

"Just a second, son. Six and seven make thirteen," corrected the coach.

"Coach, you know what? If I was as smart as you are, we'd have lost that ball game."

This is probably the truth.

In a discussion I was having with a superintendent of schools in southwest Arkansas, I mentioned that should an honor graduate leave his school and go into the world with a bad attitude, there was very little chance that that youngster would be successful.

He sat for a moment and then said sadly, "Bob, that happened to us last year."

It did not matter whether the honor student was a boy or a girl, and it mattered very little that he or she was the honor graduate. What mattered the most was that person's attitude. The application of knowledge, not the knowledge itself, made the difference.

After I spoke to a group of men at the Union Rescue Mission one Sunday afternoon, the director said, "Brother Gannaway, this may be hard for you to believe, but about a third of your audience this afternoon are college graduates, and some of these men have master's degrees."

If a college degree signifies knowledge these men had knowledge, but God love them, they were not successful.

We must take our knowledge into the mainstream and apply it. But this is not enough. Knowledge is not power; the proper use of it is power.

We can become letter-perfect in an area of knowledge and then apply that knowledge, but something very important might still be missing. Remember, *it is our attitude, not our aptitude, that will determine our altitude.* Studies suggest that about 85 percent of our failure or success in life comes from our attitudes.

If we are not happy with our position in life, all we have to do is change our attitude—our thinking—and our situation will change in direct proportion. Try it. You will be amazed to realize that you have the power and control. All you need to do is to exercise that power.

We must avoid at all costs getting trapped in the habit of measuring our achievements by others'. Playing the game of keeping up with the Joneses is the most nonproductive pastime in which we can engage.

Driving home from Kansas City, where we had attended a seminar on life after death, we were traveling through the rolling hills of southern Missouri, when Anna Mae said, "Look at that sign."

I glanced at a red and white sign advertising *Ike Shelton Insurance*. At first I saw nothing unusual about that sign, and then I remembered. For years I used the early life of Ike Shelton to illustrate a point. Had it not been a Sunday afternoon, I would have tried to find and meet him to let him know that he is one of my heroes.

As I recall his life story, when Ike was about thirteen he was stricken with polio. This was in the days when the only treatment known to doctors was isolation and rest. When the disease had run its course, Ike Shelton had a paralyzed left arm. This young man had dreamed of being a track star, and he realized that with his infirmity he would not be able to be a sprinter or a jumper but that he might be a distance runner. So he began to run. His parents enrolled him in a military school in southern Missouri. When the boys went out for track, Ike went too. He tried out for the mile run. The coach was so impressed with his determination and courage that he placed him on the track team.

When the military schools in southern Missouri came together for their final track meet, Ike Shelton represented his school in the mile event. His left arm was strapped to his body so that it would not flop and break his stride. He looked a little awkward, but there he was at the starting line with the other runners. The gun went off. Ike Shelton started and finished that race. The next morning, sportswriters wrote, "Though everyone else in the race came in ahead of him, nobody beat him."

When Ike Shelton took his place at the line he looked down the track stretching in front of him and took off and did the best he could. He did not worry about the "Joneses" in the other lanes; he just did his best. No one can do more.

It doesn't matter which way we go,
Whether east, north, south, or west;
What really matters in our lives
Is: are we doing our best?

Regardless of the talents we have,
If they be many or few,
The number is meaningless in life;
The question is, "What are we going to do?"

Will we use our blessings from God
To serve along the way,
And will we smile and lend a hand
To brighten another's dark day?

When we serve in the name of Christ
And share with others his love;
When we lift another's heavy burden
So he can raise his eyes above;

Then the stars will shine brighter for both of us,
And when life's race has been run,
We shall hear our Master's voice
Saying to us, "Well done!"

I trust that by the time you have read this far, you have found something that made you smile or maybe laugh. I also hope that you have at least one idea you can make a part of your life, so that you may fly a little higher than you have ever flown before.

I begin most of my classes by writing on the chalkboard, "If you are still breathing, you can improve," and I believe it with all my heart.

In a recent survey conducted among northern schoolchildren, it was found that nine-year-olds are already bored with life. What is happening in this great nation, the strongest, most affluent, and freest ever known, when our children are bored at age nine?

At the other end of the spectrum are those fantastic old people each of us knows, like my dear friend Eula Spivey. At age 94 she took up belly-dancing. The only reason she dropped out of the class was that poor eyesight kept her from maintaining her balance. Eula died last March in a nursing home in Springdale, Arkansas, at the age of 101.

When the entertainer Maurice Chevalier was asked at his 75th birthday party how he liked his age, he answered, "When I consider the alternatives, it's wonderful."

A 90-year-old, asked how he felt when he woke up in

the morning, replied, "Surprised."

One group I always enjoy is the XYZ Club at Immanuel Baptist Church in Little Rock, Arkansas. I have been there twenty times over the past few years. I have spoken to them, read poetry to them, and sung for them. Now I'm waiting for another invitation. I do not know what I will do, but if I am invited I intend to go. I go for what they give to me, not for what I could possibly give to them. Their love and excitement engulf Anna Mae and me each time we go. "XYZ" stands for "Extra Years of Zest."

One evening when I was speaking with them, I told them I was not sure that I could see a single middle-aged person in the audience—by my definition of middle age. There were a few snickers as I gave them that definition: *Middle age is that time of life when your broad mind and your narrow waist start changing places.*

As long as we think young, we will never grow old.

I do not believe there ever has been or ever will be a totally self-made man. You have heard about the man who is self-made—who pulled himself up by his bootstraps. I cannot accept this as the primary reason a person rises to the top. Rather, I believe what makes the difference is a waitress who gives a little child a menu and makes her feel like "people." I believe it is something that happened to a man in Russellville, Arkansas, who was retiring at the same time he was completing our motivation course. He said that when he was a teenager he was "going in the wrong direction." One day a man walked up to him and, placing his hand on his shoulder, said simply, "Son, I love you."

That is all he said, but that was enough. He told us that his life had moved pretty generally in the right direction ever since then, because one man had stopped along the way—not just to smell the roses—but to express love and concern for a teenager going in the wrong direction.

I believe it is the beauties of this great universe that you and I have a tendency to walk or drive by and never even see, which make the difference in who we become.

When I conducted three consecutive seminars about a hundred miles northwest of Little Rock, Anna Mae could go to only one of them. It was the time in the fall when the golden monarch butterflies were on their annual migration to Mexico and Central America. I took a great deal of delight in counting every single butterfly I could see; I didn't want to miss a single one. I believe it is the tears that stream down the face of a loved one, whether in joy or in sorrow, that really shape us. We become a part of all these things and they become a part of us. Let me hasten to add that I know you can put two kids on the same bench, and one of them will get off the bench and get into the game of life and make things happen, while the other youngster will move down on the other end so he can see what is going on a little better.

When you get what you want in your struggle for self
And the world makes you king for a day,
Just go to a mirror and look at yourself
And see what that man has to say.

For it isn't your father or mother or wife
Who judgment upon you must pass;
The fellow whose verdict counts most in your life
Is the one staring back from the glass.

Some people may think you a straight-shootin' chum
And call you a wonderful guy,
But the man in the glass says you're only a bum
If you can't look him straight in the eye.

He's the fellow to please, never mind the rest,
For he's with you clear up to the end.
And you've passed your most dangerous, difficult test
If the man in the glass is your friend.

You may fool the whole world down the pathway of
    years
And get pats on your back as you pass,
But your final reward will be heartaches and tears
If you've cheated the man in the glass.

—Anonymous

One of the most popular motivational messages ever recorded, "The Strangest Secret" by Earl Nightingale, tells of a preacher driving along a country road. Suddenly he came upon a beautiful farm. He was so impressed that he had to comment, and so he stopped his car and, walking over to the fence, motioned the farmer off his tractor. When the farmer approached, the preacher said, "Young man, the Lord has blessed you with a magnificent farm."

"Yes, He has," was the response, "but you should have seen this place when He had it all to Himself."

The remark gave the preacher an idea for his sermon the next Sunday. All up and down that road farmers had basically the same kind of land, but one man had made something great out of it.

You and I have something infinitely more valuable than farmland. We have a human life to live and one of God's greatest gifts, a human mind, to use. We can make something great out of it if we will just get off the bench and get into the game of life and make things happen.

Bob Gannaway has been a writer, lecturer, and seminar coordinator in the field of motivation for over thirty years. He is a native of Little Rock, Arkansas, where he lives with his wife Anna Mae.